GW01269808

Little

Written by Bob Eschenbach   Illustrated by Ruth Paul

I like to ride bikes.
So I say to my big brother,
"Can we ride bikes?"

My big brother says,
"You are too little."

I say, "I am not too little."

I like to help to fix the car.
So I say to my dad,
"Can I help to fix the car?"

My dad says,
"You are too little."

I say, "I am not too little."

I like to play with the ball.
So I say to my big sister,
"Can we play with the ball?"

My big sister says,
"You are too little."

I say, "I am not too little."

I like to help to make dinner.
So I say to my mum,
"Can I help to make dinner?"

My mum says,
"You are too little."

I say, "I am not too little."

I ask my dad
to read me a book.

He says,
"You read me a book.
You are not too little for that."

I read a book to my dad.